Better From the inside

A step to becoming an parent you want to be

By

Lucas Camila

Disclaimer:

Becoming the best parent

Becoming the best parent

Table of contents

INTRODUCTION

Try not to misunderstand me — it's great for your children to be content generally. However, there will be commonly, particularly while you're nurturing dependably, that your children will be angry.

At the point when you put down certain boundaries or give them an outcome, they dislike it at first. In any case, that is an aspect of your responsibilities depiction as a parent and top of the family. You don't settle on choices in view of what your children will like, endure, or be good with. All things being equal, you go with the choices that are best for themselves as well as your family, then see everything through to completion.

So fail to remember how blameworthy you feel. Disregard that reverberation of your sister's recommendation toward the rear of your head. Simply recall that you want to do what is best for your loved ones. You can request guidance, however eventually, you realize your family best.

Getting the Endorsement of Others

You don't require different grown-ups in that frame of mind to let you know that you are making the best decision. Nurturing isn't a ubiquity challenge in your family or locally. Of course, it feels incredible when different grown-ups, for example, your kid's instructors, let you know your kid is accomplishing something well. Yet, it's excessive for you to run your family well.

Controlling Your Children

Your kids are not manikins, and you are not a puppeteer. There is no conceivable way that you have some control over each move your kid makes or all that your kid expresses, particularly beyond your home. Kids have their own free endlessly will follow up on their own understanding — and frequently in personal circumstance.

For instance, it's essential to advise yourself that in the event that your child isn't getting her work done, notwithstanding your earnest attempts to spur her and consider her responsible, that it's her concern and the terrible score she acquires is hers alone.

The outcome she will get from you is that you will ensure she makes opportunity each night to study. You will be in contact with her educators more. Also, you will screen her schoolwork all the more completely until she brings her grade up.

Becoming the best parent

Chapter 1
Know your job

Yet, the position never accompanied sets of expectations, and no one at any point procured a school recognition or professional education in bringing up kids. The occupation is troublesome and has numerous translations. We should go through the normal ones and see where that could take us.

A Parent's Responsibility Is to Accommodate Their offspring

In the first place, guardians need to pay for things. They surrender what they had and burn through a lot of cash on things that are normally ugly, similar to diapers, child food, onesies, dens, carriages, garments and other child stuff. However, it doesn't end there. As the kid develops, their requirements change, and the old garments won't fit. We must accommodate the kid's fundamental necessities. Three of those can be dealt with cash.

Kids fundamental necessities

food

It is our obligation to take care of the children and ensure they have sufficient sustenance for improvement.

Clothes

We are liable for furnishing the children with dress that fits. It doesn't need to be a top brand, as long as the children doesn't go around stripped.

Cover

We have the obligation to give a rooftop over their heads and walls to give them security.

At the point when you move beyond diapers and crying, things begin to become fun in light of the fact that the kid will start learning new things about their current circumstance. By conversing with them and playing with them, you can show them how to talk, walk and communicate with the world. Our jobs are to train the children fundamental abilities to find actual success and respectful grown-ups. Most guardians show others how its done and change themselves and their ways of life to become positive good examples. As guardians, we are liable for educating them:

regards

We show kids how to be conscious and how to be regarded. We likewise need to assist them with learning sense of pride.

habits

We show our children fundamental habits so they don't grow up to be savage monsters.

appropriate conduct

We acquaint appropriate conduct and attempt with right conduct issues to assist them with forming into great individuals.

discipline

We show them how to have self-restraint and to do everything they can at anything they do.

Presently, except if you have a realm as a privately-owned company, it isn't our job to show them math, science and history or their inclinations. What we can do is to help them and track down the best projects for them to learn and be all that they can be in their picked fields.

Being a parent is perhaps of the main work on the planet. I figure we can all settle on that. One thing that might vary, is the main part of our parental "expected set of responsibilities." Assuming I surveyed you at this moment, I'd most likely find an alternate solution from nearly everyone. So how might we be powerful and effective as guardians on the off chance that we don't have a clue about our most significant job?

The Dad's Job

At the point when you consider the occupation of a dad, the next may ring a bell: accommodate their requirements, shield them from damage, discipline and revision, care for them, show them how to regard others, or give them daily reassurance. I'm certain you can add to the rundown. My inquiry is which one of those jobs is generally significant, or would they say they are all of equivalent significance?

The Mother's job

The occupation of the mother might cover a portion of the dad's positions. Likewise, the next may ring a bell: sustain the kids, instruct the children, energize the kids, tell them the best way to cherish, or give food and sustenance. For reasons unknown I figure the rundown of a mother's job can be significantly longer than the

12

job of a dad, as it appears to be the mother's are the essential individual with regards to kid raising and childcare. In any case all of a mother's jobs is vital, however which, if any, is generally significant?

Never center around changing your kid's way of behaving that you neglect to have a relationship with them.

I know It's disappointing to attempt to raise a dutiful and respectful child, at the end of the day, an ideal kid. One who listens when you request that they get things done, who eats their food without murmurs or grievances, and even responses yes to all that you say — the ideal kid.

I believe we're overlooking what's really important of the nurturing venture. A major piece of the excursion is to raise an individual who is conscious, kind, and a sound, useful citizen.

In the event that you have a kid who isn't submissive and getting rowdy a ton, it doesn't mean you have bombed as a parent.

Steady disciplines and letting them know how gravely they have wrecked prompts them in the end accepting what you are expecting of them: "On the off chance that I'm dependably in a difficult situation, being shouted at, and rebuffed, I should be a horrible childand I ought to simply satisfy it." How about we change that story now.
Your kid ought to hear and sense genuine love from you. Acknowledge your children as they are.

Our most significant occupation as a parent is to be cherishing while at the same time having a satisfying and significant relationship with our children.

Your relationship with your children frames the establishment for any remaining connections they will have from now on

Chapter 2

Early years matters

A child initial years can have long lasting physical, social, and close to home effects. While positive encounters and conditions can set up a small kid on a more grounded deep rooted way, horrendous encounters or conditions during those early stages can have enduring, inconvenient effect.

Youth encounters from birth to mature 8 influence the advancement of the mind's design, which gives the establishment to all future learning, conduct and wellbeing. A solid groundwork assists youngsters with fostering the abilities they need to turn out to be well-working grown-ups.

Specifically, the time among birth and age 3 is a time of quick mental health when billions of associations between individual neurons are laid out. Systems and mediations to help that improvement should be accessible start upon entering the world.

The encounters children have right off the bat in life assume a significant part in the improvement of the cerebrum. Openness to positive variables, particularly steady and responsive associations with guardians and different grown-ups, and protected and strong conditions advance positive turn of events.

At the point when mental health in babies and small kids is completely upheld, they are bound to arrive at achievements basic to future individual and local area achievement. These include:

3rd grade understanding capability
Secondary school graduation and postsecondary instruction
Productive business
Lifetime physical and psychological wellncss and prospcrity
Evasion of substance use confusion and wrongdoing

Why Early Years Matters?

Since getting the right beginning in training has an effect on kids' lives! Our point is to guarantee kids get the best open doors right from the beginning in schools and settings. We do this by advancing the prosperity and accomplishments of kids in the Early Years Establishment Stage (EYFS) and by supporting individuals who work with youngsters so together we can further develop kids' life possibilities. We generally work in principled and moral ways and we ceaselessly construct our administrations to reflect criticism. We're here to improve early training and care for youngsters!

A youngster's initial years can have long lasting physical, social, and close to home effects. While positive encounters and conditions can set up a small kid on a more grounded deep rooted way, horrendous encounters or conditions during those early stages can have enduring, inconvenient effect.

Youth encounters from birth to progress in years 8 influence the advancement of the mind's engineering, which gives the establishment to all future learning, conduct and wellbeing. A solid groundwork assists kids with fostering the abilities they need to turn out to be well-working grown-ups.

Specifically, the time among birth and age 3 is a time of fast mental health when billions of associations between individual neurons are laid out. Systems and intercessions to help that improvement should be accessible start upon entering the world.

The encounter children have right off the bat in life assume a critical part in the improvement of the mind. Openness to positive elements, particularly steady and responsive associations with guardians and different grown-ups, and protected and strong conditions advance positive turn of events.

At the point when mental health in babies and small kids is completely upheld, they are bound to arrive at achievements basic to future individual and local area achievement. These include:

Becoming the best parent

Chapter 3

Reduce shame increase connection

Disgrace happens discreetly. It doesn't injury and it doesn't scratch, and there is no undeniable look that denotes its arrival. It's not entirely obvious, and it's not difficult to figure it creates no issues. In any case, it does.

Disgrace occurs in a wide range of families, including cherishing, mindful, sustaining ones. It oversees conduct by convincing children to truly regret themselves for requiring, feeling or needing something. It is a remark about what the child is, instead of what the kid has done and it makes youngsters contract away from their true capacity, as opposed to be lighted by it.

The Issue with Disgrace.
It neglects to assist jokes around with incorporating values and illustrations.
Disgracing kids kills their ability to act from assimilated values, and on second thought starts

up their craving to avoid inconvenience just. We send them in reverse. They could make the best choice, yet inside there's no association between their way of behaving and making the best decision, 'or acting with sympathy and compassion. It makes consistent children who will act so as to keep away from future disgrace, yet it never really fabricates jokes areas of strength for with who are directed by an incorporated drive to use sound judgment. When children feel disgrace, they will zero in on what their identity is (underhanded? frustrating?), instead of what they've done.

It neglects to instruct compassion.
Sympathy is the foundation of solid connections and the capacity to understand anyone on a profound level. It expects that kids look beyond themselves to see what others may be encountering, however disgrace consumes their consideration and turns it internal on themselves and their inadequacies. We know from research that youngsters who are bound to feel disgrace really have less ability to feel compassion towards others.

It can empower socially unsuitable way of behaving.

Disgracing makes kids feel little and frail. Debilitation is something horrendous to feel and a few kids will attempt to recover this by tracking down one more method for applying their power - ordinarily by searching out somebody who is more helpless and simpler to remain over.

Models unfortunate critical thinking.

Disgracing models useless ways of managing issues. It instructs kids that it's OK to be basic, judgemental, honorable when somebody misses the point entirely. Assuming that we shout the message, it's far more terrible. A fit is a fit of rage whether it's from a grown-up or a kid. I've tossed a couple of fair ones myself, however when it works out, it's significant not to hold it out as merited or incited by the kid. Similarly we want them to possess their way of behaving, we want to do likewise.

Supports untruths and mystery.

Kids, similar to us, are wired towards self-conservation. If coming clean about a not

Becoming the best parent

exactly magnificent second will open them to disgrace, this can be sufficient motivation to stay away from reality no matter what. Assuming we believe they should come clean, we want to make it ok for them to do that.

Neglects to energize responsibility for conduct.
To change a way of behaving, there must be space to claim it. Really at that time is there extension to investigate the impacts and begin contemplating a more successful method for answering. Disgrace is bound to energize disavowal on the premise that possessing it would affirm the message of being not exactly.

What do we do all things being equal?
Youngsters normally need to satisfy individuals they care about. They'll miss the point entirely - we as a whole do - however inside them is the longing and soul to make the best decision. They will normally form into empathic, kind and aware grown-ups, yet this will require treating them with the very graciousness and regard that we anticipate from them. Disgracing can break that soul and break the association with us. The most terrible thing about this is

that it will blur our impact like it was never there regardless.

Center around the way of behaving, not the individual.
All children will do things that leave us perplexed, furious or baffled. Assuming that they're in any way similar to most of us, they won't ever stop. As opposed to saying something about them or what their identity is, ('You're so mischievous'), discuss what they've done, ('I'm profoundly vexed that you pushed your sibling. I comprehend that you're furious, yet what might have been something superior to do?'). Discipline, as in 'pupil', means to educate, and the best sort accompanies persistence, love and direction.

Grow their profound proficiency.
Having the option to get our very own feeling sentiments, as well as another person's, is a sign areas of strength for of insight. Disgrace pulverizes the potential chance to augment their close to home jargon since it clears out discourse. Exchange is gold, and there are rich open doors in any event, when things aren't

Becoming the best parent

working out in a good way. While defining limits, make serious areas of strength for a, explanation about the effect of their way of behaving, ('I'm vexed that you misled me, and I'm confounded about why you assumed you needed to.' 'I feel furious when I see you push your sibling like that. I realize you can show improvement over that'), as opposed to talking adversely about them, ('You're so devious for deceiving me'). Nothing bad can really be said about them seeing you feeling furious, annoyed or baffled in light of their way of behaving, gave you make it about their way of behaving and not about them. That is the way the world works, and you're not helping them by allowing them to figure everybody will answer the things they do with lack of interest or amazing measure. Obviously, it's significant not to be out of control in the inclination - extreme annoyance or bitterness can be terrifying for themselves and makes discussion and association basically unthinkable.

Be the individual you maintain that they should be.

They watch all that we do, and what they find in our unguarded minutes is strong. There could be no more prominent method for impacting them than to be the individual we maintain that they should be, and to answer them the manner in which we believe they should answer the world. Allow them to see consistency between what we say and what we do. In the event that we advise them to be caring and open minded, yet disgrace them when they misunderstand things, we're imparting such countless messages: 'Everybody merits consideration with the exception of you.' 'Children must be thoughtful yet adults can be anything.' 'It's OK to be unkind to more modest individuals.' For a little individual (or a major one), it doesn't get significantly more confounding than that.

Treat them like they are now the individual you maintain that they should be.

Each time we associate with them, we're forming the picture they have of themselves. That picture is so strong - they'll satisfy it or down to it. We need to protect their identity and keep the picture of themselves as entire, unblemished, innovative, able, strong, solid,

Becoming the best parent

wonderful creatures. We additionally believe that they should see themselves as sincerely dependable. This is so significant. Lifting them up, and sustaining their feeling of individual strengthening, without showing them the effect of their conduct on individuals risks raising little egomaniacs who are perpetually getting their own requirements met to the detriment of every other person's. We can sustain the picture inside them by regarding them like they are now individuals we maintain that they should be, 'I realize you are a truly mindful individual and you wouldn't hurt individuals deliberately. We should discuss what coincidentally knew.' 'that you didn't plan to make your sister feel awful, yet that what happens when mean things are said. How might you put this right?' What we take care of will become significant, so on the off chance that we can pump the brakes to the point of seeing them through their way of behaving, we will illuminate the individual they are equipped for becoming.

 Marks can occur with such ease and in spite of the fact that they are much of the time finished with affection and good motivations, they can blow up. In the event that one childis known as, say, 'the energetic one' or 'the entertaining one', different kids in the family could decipher themselves as 'not the lively one' or 'not the amusing one'. Nothing bad can really be said about let kids know how much fun they are or the amount you love watching them do their thing on the games field, yet we need complex children who make up their own personalities about their assets and shortcomings, and who will have a go at a lot of things, whether it ends up being 'their thing' or not.

Try not to purchase into the examinations.
It's so natural to become involved with the madness - and it can feel like panic - about where your own kid sits comparable to different children in the grade, the group, the music class - or anything that it is they're in. Watch out for those parent all-in visits where every other person's kid is by all accounts concentrating such a ton harder than yours, perusing Shakespeare while yours is staggering over Peppa Pig, or paying attention to Mozart while yours is paying attention to the sound that happens when they suck on a straw and the glass goes void. They'll have their own assets

and they'll track down their own specific manners to sparkle. It very well may be in totally unforeseen manner and they probably won't track down it for some time - and that is fine. Meanwhile, give them the opportunity to investigate without compelling them to be something they're not. Empower them down various tracks, and support their work, however miss the mark regarding looking at them. Conversing with different guardians can set off our own disgrace around being 'sufficient' guardians. I feel like I'm continually grappling with this one. Manage it and put it where it should be, however don't give it to the children. Make a stride back and see them for the entire, wonderful, special individuals they are. At times, it's the things they do any other way to every other person that end up being their inconceivable assets.

Be available to the things they do that are an ordinary piece of their development.
Similarly that as a feature of our development and advancing as guardians we will get things fabulously off-base, so too will our youngsters. Little kids are interested and conceited. They

29

were constructed that method for giving them what they need to investigate the world and how everything affects them. Youngsters may be unfriendly or not interested in our impact and appear to push against us purposely. This gives them what they

Becoming the best parent

Chapter 4

building connection capital

The main relationship to a childis the one they create with their parent or guardian. Youngsters find out about their general surroundings through a positive parent-kid relationship. As they are developing and changing, youngsters focus on their folks to decide if they are protected, secure, and cherished. It is additionally the establishment from which they will fabricate their future connections.

You can construct a good parent-kid relationship by being at the time with your kid, getting to know each other, and establishing a climate where they feel great to investigate. There is no mysterious handbook or dependable way to deal with get this relationship right, and you'll probably track down difficulties en route. Nonetheless, assuming that you continue dealing with working on your relationship, your kid will clearly bloom.

Keep perusing for eight positive-nurturing strategies that can assist you with reinforcing the connection among you and your kid:

ways to build strong connection with children

Show Your Affection

Human touch and cherishing love is required at each phase of our lives for solid profound and neurobiological turn of events. Your kid must get delicate, adoring touch (i.e., embraces) from you a few times over the course of the day. Treat each communication as a chance to interface with your kid. Welcome them with warm articulations, give eye to eye connection, grin, and energize fair association.

Say "I love you" frequently
It is much of the time inferred that we love our kids, yet make certain to let them know consistently, regardless of what age they are. In any event, when your kid is being troublesome

or accomplishes something you could do without; this can be a great chance to advise them that you love them genuinely. A straightforward "I love you" can significantly affect your drawn out relationship with your kid.

Put down stopping points, rules, and results Youngsters need design and direction as they develop and find out about their general surroundings. Converse with your kids about what you expect of them and ensure they comprehend. At the point when rules are broken, make a point to have age-suitable results set up and be predictable with them. To become familiar with age-fitting results,

Tune in and understand

Association begins with tuning in. Recognize your kid's sentiments, show them you comprehend, and console them that you are there to assist with anything they need. Attempt to see things according to your kid's viewpoint. By tuning in and sympathizing with your kid, you will start to encourage common regard.

Play Together

Play means a lot to a youngster's turn of events. It is the instrument through which kids foster language abilities, express feelings, encourage inventiveness, and find out about interactive abilities. Moreover, it is a pleasant way for you to reinforce your relationship with your kid. It doesn't make any difference what you play. The key is to simply partake in one another and focus on truly focusing on your kid.

Play Isn't Only for Youngsters

Training

Want to come join in the festivities? This sincere youth greeting to draw in with companions is perceived all over the planet by individuals, everything being equal. Play falls into place without a hitch for most kids since it is their picked language to convey. Youngsters begin to play when they are babies - associating with their reality through development and finding how their body moves. As a childages, they take part in different sorts of play as they notice and cooperate with others. Language, social, and engine improvement are upgraded by both coordinated and free play. It's pivotal to our emotional well-being too.

Is it safe to say that you are as yet playing? A large portion of us begin tracking down different exercises to keep us occupied as we create and mature. As grown-ups, the most we play may be a stage recording walk, a tabletop game with a youngster, and perhaps a computer game. Not the sort of play we did as children, and not exactly that much fun by the same token. Tracking down ways of consolidating play in our ordinary routine might help us in various ways, particularly all through this pandemic.

Play isn't only for youngsters any longer, and it very well may be the distinct advantage to remain youthful on a basic level! Communicating with others and freeing ourselves up to appreciating exercises right now permits us to improve our nearest connections as well as foster new ones. At the point when guardians model positive interactive abilities during play, children can acquire new abilities and improve the ones they have, such as

Becoming the best parent

alternating and having persistence. By conveying and associating with others, we constantly foster new interactive abilities and reinforce lively perspectives all through our lifetime.

Play, in many structures, further develops mind capability, from riddles and memory games to actual play that gets the old heart siphoning. That old legend that the mind is set early on is totally bogus. Brain adaptability is the idea that our cerebrum continues developing and changing all through our lifetime. Brain processes are animated through play exercises and can make new synaptic associations. Innovativeness gets a lift from play where we make, move, decide and involve our creative mind in something like Prisons and Winged serpents, a fanciful casual get-together or even a 30-second dance party. Sharing tomfoolery and being energetic assists us with creating sympathy, compassion, trust, and closeness. Laughter is a pain reliever with no side effects, so a rowdy round of pretenses may be exactly what was needed

Different ways Families Can Utilize Play to Assemble Association and Having a place

1. Make Ordinary Assignments Into Games

Now and again the consistently undertakings, errands, and obligations we have as families become repetitive. Loads of families experience obstruction from kids (and perhaps guardians) with regards to these undertakings. At the point when the dull errands are transformed into games, it gives an open door to association and fun as a family. Perhaps you transform cleaning the house into a dance party by turning up your number one tunes. Collapsing clothing can be changed into a game about who can find the most sock matches. Transform getting toys into a competition to see who can put five toys into the container first.

2. Have 15 Minutes Every Day be Saved for Exceptional Association Time

Research shows that having only 15 minutes of uniquely held time for guardians and youngsters to interface can work on confidence, assemble connections, and lessening testing ways of behaving. During a unique association time, it's critical that guardians are totally present - no telephones, no interruptions. Children ought to likewise be the forerunners in what's going on during this exceptional association time. Does the childneed to variety? Then, at that point, variety. Would they like to play dolls? Play dolls. Utilizing good non-verbal correspondence, eye to eye connection, and being close in nearness will assist kids with feeling extraordinary and really focused on.

3. Incorporate Perky Customs and Schedules into Your Day

Customs are examples of collaborations or extraordinary occasions that have a particular importance and underline association. For instance, an extraordinary cradlesong that is sung consistently can be a custom. During supper, perhaps you generally discuss a "rose and a thistle" from the day or a "cheerful thing and something horrible" from the day. Everybody will share and everybody pays attention to each other. Perhaps you have an extraordinary handshake you use with your kid. Significantly, it has meaning and is done routinely as a piece of your family's social rhythms.

Through purposeful, energetic, and dreary social rhythms, solid relationship examples and abilities can be created by individuals, everything being equal. Fostering these solid social rhythms don't need to be hard to incorporate into your ordinary, day to day existence. Partake in being together by utilizing play inside your loved ones!

Be accessible and interruption free
Saving only 10 minutes per day to converse with to your youngster, without interruptions, can have a major effect in laying out great correspondence propensities. Switch off the television, set aside your electronic gadgets, and get to know one another. Your kid has to realize that you accept they are fundamentally

important in your life regardless of the numerous interruptions and stressors that come your direction.

Eat dinners together

Eating all together can frequently prompt incredible discussion and holding time with your youngster. Urge everybody to take care of their telephones or different gadgets and essentially appreciate each other's conversation. Dinner time is likewise an extraordinary chance for you to show your kids the significance of a sound and adjusted diet, which likewise impacts their in general psychological wellness.

Make parent-kid ceremonies

In the event that you have more than one kid, attempt to try investing individual energy with every one of them. Quality, one-on-one time with your childcan fortify the parent-kid bond, develops your kid's confidence, and tells them that they are extraordinary and esteemed. A few guardians plan for extraordinary "date evenings" with their youngsters to make that one-on-a single an open door (whether it's a stroll around the area, an excursion to the jungle gym, or simply a film at home - it's essential to separately praise every kid).

Becoming the best parent

Becoming the best parent

Chapter 5

not listening

Tuning in, for what it's worth, is something troublesome. What's more, to consider paying attention to your childappears to be an overwhelming undertaking. Is it vital to pay attention to your youngster? Add to that the way that when the kid should be paid attention to, you might have another 1000 things running at the forefront of your thoughts needing you to simply leap off your seat at this moment.

Notwithstanding, research expresses that paying attention to your children causes it more probable that they to pay attention to you (which the majority of us need). At the point when a childfeels paid attention to, he is bound to tune in, and having been perceived, he will comprehend your perspective as well. It assists guardians and kids with framing more grounded bonds and connections, and fabricates their confidence.

The Rudiments of Paying attention to Your Kid

Talking and paying attention to your childhold a ton of significance. It assists your kid with building a bond with you and foster his confidence in you. Listening works on the holding in a relationship and fabricates a youngster's certainty. Very few guardians have the expertise to 'tune in', yet with a cognizant exertion, they can foster it. What's more, gradually, with training, you can dominate it also.

At the point when you are attempting to talk or speak with your kid, you should:Encourage your kid to open dependent upon you by talking.
Be patient and pay attention to your kid while he puts his sentiments and considerations across.
According to answer in a delicate manner to all that he, positive or negative.
Center around non-verbal communication and activities in order to grasp the non-verbal types of his correspondence.
[Peruse: Correspondence A Specialty of Connecting]

How Could I as a Parent Further develop My Listening Abilities?
How Might I as a Parent Further develop My Listening Skills_

Listening is definitely not a simple errand. As a parent, you will feel enticed to speak more loudly and tell your kid they are off-base. It takes a ton of persistence to sincerely hear out somebody, not to mention a kid, as you might get to hear something that you are disturbed about.

Your kid might offer something that challenges your view or convictions, or you might hear something that will make you need to change, or it might disturb your thought process. Furthermore, for that reason it is critical to foster listening abilities in yourself first, prior to getting your kid to converse with you. Furthermore, how would you do this?

Practice undivided attention and spotlight on the thing the kid is attempting to say without shaping or offering any viewpoints.

Place yourself from your kid's perspective, envision the way in which you would have responded in a given circumstance that your kid is in.

Be available actually and intellectually. At the point when you get your kid to talk, be completely at the time. The dishes can stand by, so can your calls. Tell your childthey stand out enough to be noticed.

Notice your kid's non-verbal communication and translate the non-verbal things your childis attempting to say.

Show interest and have a receptive outlook. You ought not be critical with regards to paying attention to any one

What are the Adverse consequences of Not Paying attention to Your Youngster?

Without you being even mindful of it, your everyday conduct influences your kid in numerous ways, molding their future character. As guardians, you impact your kid's life purposefully or unexpectedly or both.

From your manner of speaking to the words you pick, your kid masters the abilities important to interface with you - as guardians are basically a kid's most memorable instructor. Youngsters who are not heard turned into the ones who won't ever tune in. They will constantly be mostly certain, hopefully not by mistake, that they are contemptible of your time and consideration.

Anything they do, think, or feel is negative. They lose certainty and confidence, which can be negative to their advancement as youthful grown-ups. A childwho is frequently judged or condemned loses interest in sharing and conveying and turns out to be packaged, alone, and unapproachable.

Hints on Conversing with Your Kid and Pay attention to them

A few children are normally expressive, and they work everything out, while others might require a great deal of consolation to have the option to talk with you. The main thing is to be available to tuning in and truly focus on your kid.

Here are a few hints on getting your kid to converse with you and be available to tuning in:

Put away Some Quality Time:

Put away when you both can converse with one another with next to no impedance. If up close and personal talk appears to be troublesome, take a walk and get some margin to visit. Else, take your childfor a drive and allow them to sit in the secondary lounge and have a discussion.

Stay away from Pre-defined Limits

Be responsive and open to a wide range of sentiments without blowing up or baffled. Recall that discussions won't generally be positive, yet in addition incorporate negative themes like displeasure, dread and uneasiness.

Come at the situation from Their Perspective

Recall that youngsters really do have similar development as grown-ups do. Consider the times when you were a kid and that it was so challenging to convey when you have such a lot of running to you yet need more words.

Persistence is the Key

Try not to be in that frame of mind to answer. Allow your kid to get done with talking and afterward answer delicately. At the point when your childis talking, don't bounce in or meddle. Never attempt to make assumptions for your youngster. Never under any circumstance holler.

Never Talk Your Youngster

Abstain from addressing. Addressing is one approach to putting your view across, while a drawing in discussion cultivates their own reasoning cycle and ends.

Make Moving Discussions

Make the discussions, motivating for your kid. Stories are an ideal method for rousing small children. Continuously underscore the positive.

Be careful with Language

Use language that your childwill get it. Try not to utilize words that they might see as challenging to fathom. Try not to utilize shoptalk or convoluted words - talk similarly as your childdoes.

Listen Cautiously

Tell your kid that you are paying attention to them. Rehash what they say and visually connect. Show your advantage in the discussion. Being effectively engaged with the discussion is critical to tell your kid that his perspectives and conclusions matter.

Never Judge the youngster

Never judge, reprimand, fault or fly off the handle over something that your kid has done or said. Cooperate collectively to tackle your concerns.

At the point when you stand by listening to your kid, you get to understand what they are thinking, feeling, and going through. Youth is a troublesome stage, and with restricted jargon, kids frequently find it hard to convey their sentiments.

Kids actually must be heard so they don't contain their sentiments. It likewise implies that your kids will pay attention to you more since they have been heard. This opens up roads for solid discussions, which are productive and bring guardians and youngsters closer

Chapter 6

lying

We show our children that lying is wrong, however we've all probably told our children harmless embellishments. Like the time you let them know the jungle gym was shut when truly you simply needed to return home. Or on the other hand when you advised your children that assuming they keep on making that face, it will be stuck like that until the end of time. These untruths might appear to be innocuous, however a few specialists concur that the falsehoods we tell our youngsters currently could affect their way of behaving as grown-ups.

As per another review distributed in the Diary of Exploratory childBrain science, misleading our children makes adverse impacts and can prompt our kids lying when they become grown-ups.

For the review, scientists found out if their folks deceived them when they were youngsters, the amount they lie to their folks currently and how well they change in accordance with adulthood challenges. What they found was that members who said they were in many cases deceived as kids were bound to mislead their folks now. These members additionally announced confronting more noteworthy trouble in gathering mental and social difficulties, said they encountered culpability and disgrace, and depicted themselves as being egotistical and manipulative.

"Nurturing by lying can appear to save time, particularly when the genuine explanations for why guardians believe that youngsters should do something is muddled to make sense of," lead creator and Partner Teacher Setoh Peipei said. "At the point when guardians let youngsters know that 'genuineness is the smartest strategy', yet show deceitfulness by lying, such way of behaving can send contradictory signals to their kids. Guardians' contemptibility may ultimately disintegrate trust and advance untruthfulness in youngsters."

A significant number of the members said the falsehoods depended on basic points like eating, leaving or potentially remaining, the kid getting out of hand and cash.

Specialists of the review said that they trust these outcomes help guardians "think about options in contrast to lying, for example, recognizing youngsters' sentiments, giving data so kids know what's in store, offering decisions and critical thinking together."

Thus, the following time you ponder telling your children an innocent embellishment, make sure to try to do you say others should do — genuineness truly is the smartest strategy.

Why innocent exaggerations are hurtful
Innocent exaggerations appear to be innocuous and it could feel that there is nothing out of sorts in utilizing them on occasion when you are trapped in a tough spot. By the by, another review conveyed by the specialists in Singapore uncovered that being even somewhat exploitative with children can influence our children unfavorably. Your clarification could

Becoming the best parent

persuade them for some time, however it might adversely affect your little one. They are bound to lie when they grow up and may try and experience issues managing mental and social difficulties Reinforcing the parent-kid connections requires work and exertion. Nurturing is a difficult situation, yet by keeping a cozy relationship and open correspondence with kids, guardians can remain associated with them during all phases of life.

Further, serious areas of strength for a kid association really makes nurturing simpler, since youngsters who feel more associated with their folks are more disposed to tune in, help and follow directions.1 Youngsters who feel associated likewise are more able to converse with their folks about issues with companions or in school. The following are 10 methods for extending connections among guardians and youngsters.
9

Tell kids you love them consistently, regardless of their age. Indeed, even on attempting days or after conflicts, guardians ought to ensure kids know that in spite of the fact that you could have done without their way of behaving, you love them unconditionally.

Struggle is the main time for guardians to convey their adoration to their kids. A basic "I love you" does burdens to reinforce connections.

Allow your children to see your senseless side. More seasoned kids appreciate cards, chess, and PC games, while more youthful ones have a great time playing any game with guardians.
Lay out a Unique Name or Code Word
Make a unique name for your kid that is positive or a mystery code word that you can use with one another. Utilize the name as a basic support of your adoration. The code word can be utilized to remove a kid from an awkward circumstance, (for example, a sleepover that isn't working out positively) without making excessive shame the kid.

Create and Keep up with Sleep time Customs
Perusing sleep time books or recounting stories to kids makes deep rooted ceremonies. Sleep time is a partition and making a ceremonial

causes children to feel safer.4 Sleep time may likewise be the main time working guardians share with their children; make it quiet and charming.

When kids begin perusing, have them perused a page, section, or short book to you. Indeed, even most young people actually partake in the custom of being told goodnight in an extraordinary manner by a parent.

Show Your Children Confidence.
Show your kid your confidence and convictions. Let them know what you accept and why. Permit time for your childto sincerely get clarification on pressing issues and respond to them. Support those lessons frequently.

Chapter 7

Building confidence

Here and there it's not difficult to see when children appear to feel better about themselves, and when they don't. We frequently portray this thought of having a decent outlook on ourselves as "confidence."

Jokes around with confidence:

feel preferred and acknowledged
feel sure
feel pleased with what they can do
think beneficial things about themselves
have faith in themselves
Messes with low confidence:

are self-basic and hard on themselves
fecl they're not comparable to different children

consider the times they bomb as opposed to when they succeed
need certainty
question they can do things effectively
Why Confidence Matters
Kids who feel better about themselves have the certainty to attempt new things. They are bound to make an honest effort. They feel glad for what they can do. Confidence assists jokes with adapting to botches. It assists messes around with attempting once more, regardless of whether they fizzle right away. Therefore, confidence assists jokes with improving at school, at home, and with companions.

Jokes around with low confidence feel uncertain of themselves. On the off chance that they figure others will not acknowledge them, they may not participate. They might allow others to mistreat them. They might struggle with defending themselves. They might surrender effectively, or not attempt by any means. Jokes with low confidence find it hard to adapt when they commit an error, lose, or fall flat. Thus, they may not work out quite as well as they could.

How Confidence Creates

Confidence can begin as soon as infancy. It grows gradually after some time. It can begin in light of the fact that a kid has a real sense of security, cherished, and acknowledged. It can begin when a child stands out and cherishing care.

As infants become babies and small kids, they're ready to do a few things without anyone else. They feel significantly better about themselves when they can utilize their new abilities. Their confidence develops when guardians focus, let a kid attempt, give grins, and show they're pleased.

As children develop, confidence can develop as well. Any time kids attempt things, get things done, and learn things can be an opportunity for confidence to develop. This can happen when kids:

gain ground toward an objective
learn things at school
make companions and get along

master abilities — music, sports, craftsmanship, cooking, tech abilities

practice most loved exercises

help, give, or be thoughtful

get acclaim for good ways of behaving

make a good attempt at something

do things they're great at and appreciate

are incorporated by others

feel got it and acknowledged

get an award or a passing mark they realize they've procured

At the point when children have confidence, they feel sure, fit, and acknowledged for what their identity is.

How Guardians Can Construct Confidence

Each kid is unique. Confidence might come more straightforward to certain children than others. Furthermore, a few children face things that can bring down their confidence. In any case, regardless of whether a youngster's confidence is low, it tends to be raised.

Here are things guardians can do to assist jokes with having a decent outlook on themselves:

Assist your kid with figuring out how to get things done. At each age, there are new things for youngsters to learn. In any event, during diaper days, figuring out how to hold a cup or make first strides starts a feeling of dominance and joy. As your childdevelops, things like figuring out how to dress, read, or ride a bicycle are opportunities for confidence to develop.

While showing kids how to get things done, show and help them from the start. Then, at that point, let them give their best, regardless of whether they commit errors. Be certain your kid has an opportunity to learn, attempt, and feel pleased. Try not to make new difficulties excessively simple — or excessively hard.

Acclaim your youngster, however do it shrewdly. Obviously, applauding kids is great. Your commendation is a method for showing that you're glad. However, a few different ways of commending children can really blow up.

This is the way to get everything done as needs be:

Try not to overpraise. Acclaim that doesn't feel acquired doesn't sound accurate. For instance, telling a childhe played an extraordinary game when he realizes he didn't feels empty and phony. It's smarter to say, "I realize that wasn't your best game, yet we as a whole have off days. I'm glad for you for not surrendering." Add a demonstration of positive support: "Tomorrow, you'll be back on your game."

Acclaim exertion. Try not to zero in acclaim just on results, (for example, getting A) or fixed characteristics, (for example, being brilliant or athletic).

All things being equal, offer a large portion of your commendation for exertion, progress, and disposition. For instance: "You're buckling down on that task," "You're getting endlessly better at these spelling tests," or, "I'm glad for you for rehearsing piano — you've truly stayed with it." With this sort of commendation, kids put exertion into things, make progress toward objectives, and attempt. At the point when that's what children do, they're bound to succeed.

Be a decent good example. At the point when you put exertion into regular undertakings (like raking the leaves, making a feast, tidying up the dishes, or washing the vehicle), you're setting a genuine model. Your childfigures out how to invest energy into doing schoolwork, tidying up toys, or making the bed.

Demonstrating the right disposition counts as well. At the point when you take care of assignments happily (or if nothing else without protesting or whining), you train your kid to do likewise. At the point when you try not to race through errands and invest wholeheartedly in nicely done, you help your kid to do that as well.

Boycott unforgiving analysis. The messages kids catch wind of themselves from others effectively convert into how they feel about themselves. Brutal words ("That is no joke!") are hurtful, not inspiring. At the point when children hear negative messages about themselves, it hurts their confidence. Right children with tolerance. Center around what you maintain that they should do sometime later. When required, show them how.

Becoming the best parent

Center around qualities. Focus on what your kid gets along nicely and appreciates. Ensure your kid has opportunities to foster these qualities. Center more around qualities than shortcomings to assist jokes with having a decent outlook on themselves. This further develops conduct as well.

Allow children to help and give. Confidence develops when children get to see that what they do matters to other people. Children can assist at home, do a help project at school, or help out for a kin. Aiding and kind demonstrations fabricate confidence and other nice sentiments.

Hints on building confidence in kids

Basically commending your kid can really cause more damage than great. Here is a far reaching guide on the most proficient method to construct fearlessness in a youngster.

Last week, my child Aaron made the school soccer group. Kid, was I pleased. Furthermore, I was unable to quit saying as much. "Great job, pal! You're really amazing!" I radiated, he radiated, and everything appeared to be ok with the world.

It's not whenever my children first have heard me yell their gestures of recognition. I'm the occupant cheering segment, their most diehard follower, a back-patter professional. Nowadays, you can find me distributing praises as though they're sticks of gum — when my children practice guitar, score an objective, assist with dishes. The mother rationale goes this way: The childaccomplishes something useful (or adequate for me), so I help him have a positive outlook on himself. It's called supporting confidence. Or on the other hand so I thought. Here are a few things you might not have thought about regarding building confidence in kids.

1. Step back

For reasons unknown, there are better ways of building confidence than loading on acclaim for all that children do — beginning with assisting them with becoming equipped on the planet, says Jim Taylor, writer of the book Your

Becoming the best parent

Children Are Tuning in: Nine Messages They Need to Hear from You. To do as such, however, you need to figure out how to step back and let your kid otake gambles, simply decide, tackle issues and stick with what they start.

Commercial

2. Over-adulating kids causes more damage than great

Confidence comes from feeling cherished and secure, and from creating ability, Taylor says, and in spite of the fact that guardians frequently give their children the initial two fixings, capability — turning out to be great at things — takes time and exertion. "However much we probably will need to, we can't commend our children into ability," he says.

As a matter of fact, by over-commending kids, we're causing more damage than great. "We're bringing down the bar for them," Taylor says. "In the event that you continue to tell your kid she is now working effectively, you're saying she never again needs to propel herself. However, certainty comes from doing, from

Becoming the best parent

falling flat and attempting once more — from training."

Samantha MacLeod, who has four young men, ages one to nine, accepts consistent praising can really dissolve confidence. Either kids begin believing they're awesome or they attempt to be amazing constantly — a unimaginable norm. Also, wrong recognition confounds them, she says. "In the event that my child can't spell and I let him know he's doing tremendous, he learns not to trust his own senses. He additionally discovers that recognition is only absolutely lying."

Also, Taylor adds, telling your childhe's awesome, the savviest or the most skilled is setting him up for some extremely terrible news not too far off. You're making an egomaniac who thinks his scrawls are Rothkos at the same time, sometime, he'll find he's not exactly all things considered.

Promotion
3. Allow your chil dto face solid challenges

Begin by compelling yourself to remain back while your childfaces solid challenges, says Victoria Sopik, President of Children and Company, a corporate childcare administration in Toronto, and a mother of eight. "To assemble trust on the planet, kids need to take risks, simply decide and get a sense of ownership with them," Sopik says. She sees an excessive number of guardians attempting to protect their children from disappointment constantly.

Sopik gazed from across the room as her two-year-old child, Fraser, lifted a gigantic container of orange pop at an extravagant party. "He was going to empty it into a glass, and I just remained there, pausing my breathing," Sopik reviews. As opposed to attempting to save her child before he got an opportunity to attempt, Sopik looked as Fraser spilled the pop all around the floor.

Then came the most outstanding aspect: Fraser tracked down a server, requested a paper towel and tidied up his own wreck. "He tackled his own concern — very much as we do as effective grown-ups," Sopik says.

4. Allow children to go with their own decisions
At the point when children pursue their own age-suitable decisions, they feel all the more impressive, says Sopik, bringing up that children as youthful as two can begin thinking about the outcomes of their choices.

Becoming the best parent